WeightWatchers®
pure points

Recipes for

5 Points and under

Over 40 recipes low in points

Edited by Sue Beveridge

SIMON & SCHUSTER
A VIACOM COMPANY

First published in Great Britain by
Simon & Schuster UK Ltd, 2002
A Viacom Company

Copyright © 2002, Weight Watchers International, Inc.

All the recipes in this book have been published
previously by Weight Watchers.

Simon & Schuster UK Ltd
Africa House
64–78 Kingsway
London
WC2B 6AH

Editorial project manager: Anna Hitchin
Photography and styling by Tim Auty
Food preparation by Becky Johnson
Design by Jane Humphrey
Typesetting by Stylize Digital Artwork
Printed and bound in Hong Kong

Weight Watchers Publications Manager: Corrina Griffin
Weight Watchers Publications Executive: Lucy Davidson
Weight Watchers Editor: Sue Beveridge

A CIP catalogue for this book is available from the
British Library

ISBN 0 743 23093 0

Pictured on the front cover: Turkey Tomato Pasta, page 44
Pictured on the back cover: Banana Bread, page 49

All eggs, fruit and vegetables are medium-size unless
otherwise stated; teaspoons (5 ml) and tablespoons
(15 ml) are level.

V denotes a vegetarian recipe and assumes vegetarian
cheese and free-range eggs are used. Virtually fat-free
fromage frais and low-fat crème fraîche may contain traces
of gelatine so they are not always vegetarian: please check
the labels.

contents

Introduction   **4**

1 point and under   **5**

2 points and under   **17**

3 points and under   **27**

4 points and under   **39**

5 points and under   **51**

Index   **63**

Do you ever wish you had more points in a day? Do you ever wish you could prepare filling meals that would still leave you enough points for a treat? Then this cookbook has been written especially for you!

There are lots of mouth-watering recipes that are both filling and low in points. Every recipe has been chosen specifically because it's low in points and tastes great. You won't find any recipes with more than 5 points, and over half of them have 3 points or less.

So now you can make your points go further. You'll feel full and satisfied on a minimum of points without having to compromise on portion size, flavour or enjoyment. And, when you do have 1 or 2 points to spare, browsing through the pages of this book will give you plenty of tasty ideas for turning those extra points into something really special.

The recipes are grouped into chapters by the points per serving, and in each chapter you'll find a wide selection of filling main meals, tasty snacks and delicious desserts and bakes. Every recipe gives you details on preparation and cooking times, freezing information and of course points per serving and per recipe. Recipes suitable for vegetarians are also clearly marked.

Here you'll find the lowest point collection of recipes we have ever published so with *pure points*™, it need no longer just be a fantasy to enjoy a delicious doughnut for just ½ a point (page 13), or a satisfying casserole for 3 points (page 33).

1 point
and under

Zero point soup

Butternut squash soup

Mushroom curry

Oven-roasted tomato tartlets

Moroccan vegetable stew

Grilled vegetable kebabs with a hot
   tomato glaze

Baked doughnuts

Cookies

Apple drop scones

Toffee apple wedges

serves: **4**   preparation: **10** mins   cooking: **15** mins

POINTS PER SERVING

0

points per recipe
0

- **2 vegetable stock cubes, dissolved in 1 litre (1¾ pints) hot water**
- **a bunch of spring onions, trimmed and sliced finely**
- **1 carrot, cut into fine strips**
- **1 teaspoon Thai seven-spice seasoning**
- **1 leek, shredded finely**
- **1 small courgette, shredded finely**
- **1 small red or yellow pepper, de-seeded and shredded finely**
- **50 g (1¾ oz) Savoy or white cabbage, shredded coarsely**
- **a pinch of dried red chilli flakes (optional)**
- **salt and freshly ground black pepper**
- **1 tablespoon chopped fresh coriander or parsley, to garnish**

Zero point soup

V

1 Pour the stock into a large saucepan and add the spring onions and carrot. Bring to the boil, then cover and reduce the heat. Simmer for 5 minutes.

2 Add the Thai seven-spice seasoning, leek, courgette, pepper and cabbage. Add the red chilli flakes, if using, replace the lid and bring back to a simmer. Simmer for a further 5 minutes.

3 Season to taste, then ladle the soup into warm bowls and serve, garnished with chopped fresh coriander or parsley.

Freezing not recommended

Butternut squash soup

POINTS PER SERVING

0

points per recipe
0

1 Put the squash and onion into a large saucepan and add the stock and the spices.

2 Bring to the boil, cover, then reduce the heat and simmer for about 20 minutes until the squash is tender.

3 Transfer the soup to a liquidiser or food processor and blend until smooth.

4 Return to the saucepan and reheat gently. Season to taste, then serve garnished with the chopped parsley.

Freezing recommended

- **1 small butternut squash, peeled, de-seeded and chopped**
- **1 onion, chopped**
- **1 vegetable stock cube, dissolved in 600 ml (1 pint) hot water**
- **½ teaspoon ground cumin**
- **½ tablespoon ground coriander**
- **salt and freshly ground black pepper**
- **1 tablespoon of fresh chopped parsley, to garnish**

- **low-fat cooking spray**
- **2 onions, sliced**
- **300 g (10½ oz) mixed mushrooms (e.g. button, chestnut, oyster), sliced thickly or halved depending on size**
- **2 garlic cloves, crushed**
- **2 teaspoons medium-strength curry powder**
- **½ teaspoon cumin seeds**
- **3 tablespoons tomato purée**
- **4 tablespoons low-fat plain bio yogurt**
- **½ teaspoon ground fenugreek (optional)**
- **salt and freshly ground black pepper**

Mushroom curry

V

1 Heat a non-stick pan and spray with the low-fat cooking spray. Stir-fry the onions for about 8 minutes until soft and brown.

2 Reduce the heat, add the rest of the ingredients to the pan and heat gently until the mushrooms start to release their juices. Cover the pan with a tight-fitting lid and simmer for 10 minutes, stirring regularly.

3 Remove the lid and continue cooking for a minute or two, then season to taste and serve.

Freezing not recommended

Oven-roasted tomato tartlets

POINTS PER TARTLET

1

points per recipe
10

V

1 Preheat the oven to Gas Mark 2/150°C/fan oven 130°C.

2 Arrange the tomatoes cut-side up on a cooling rack. Place the cooling rack over a baking sheet then sprinkle the salt over the tomatoes.

3 Roast the tomatoes in the oven for 1 hour, until they are beginning to dry out a little.

4 Remove them from the oven and increase the oven temperature to Gas Mark 5/190°C/fan oven 170°C. Cut each sheet of filo pastry in half, brush with oil and place the two halves together with the corners at angles to each other – not neatly lined up in a square. Gently press into 8 individual tartlet tins scrunching up the edges with your fingers so the pastry fits into the tins. Brush the insides of the tartlet cases with any remaining oil. Bake for 10–15 minutes, until the pastry is crisp and golden.

5 Remove from the oven then carefully lift the pastry cases from the tins and place on serving plates. Fill with the roasted tomato halves. Scatter each tartlet with a little torn basil, if using, and a generous grinding of black pepper.

Freezing recommended for the roasted tomatoes only

- **1 kg (2 lb 4 oz) plum tomatoes, halved horizontally**
- **1 teaspoon salt**
- **8 sheets of filo pastry**
- **2 tablespoons olive oil**
- **2 tablespoons torn fresh basil leaves (optional)**
- **freshly ground black pepper**

serves: **2**   preparation: **30** mins + **15** mins standing   cooking: **30** mins

points per recipe
1½

- **1 small aubergine, sliced thinly**
- **1 red pepper**
- **1 green pepper**
- **2 teaspoons olive oil**
- **1 onion, sliced**
- **1 garlic clove, crushed**
- **1 fresh red chilli, de-seeded and chopped**
- **1 teaspoon ground cumin**
- **225 g (8 oz) plum tomatoes, skinned, de-seeded and chopped**
- **150 ml (¼ pint) vegetable stock or tomato juice**
- **salt and freshly ground black pepper**
- **2 tablespoons chopped fresh coriander, to garnish**

Moroccan vegetable stew

V

1 Place the aubergine in a colander, sprinkling each layer with salt. Cover with a weighted plate and leave to stand for 15 minutes, then rinse and drain thoroughly.

2 Place the peppers under a hot grill, turning frequently, until the skin is charred and blistered. Put in a plastic bag and leave to cool.

3 Heat the oil in a saucepan, add the onion, garlic and chilli and cook gently for 5 minutes, until softened but not coloured. Add the cumin and cook for 1 minute more.

4 Halve the aubergine slices and add to the pan then add the tomatoes and stock or tomato juice. Season with pepper. Simmer for 20 minutes, partly covered, stirring occasionally.

5 Meanwhile, peel the peppers, discarding the cores and seeds. Cut the flesh into thin strips.

6 Five minutes before the end of cooking, stir the pepper strips into the aubergine mixture. Season to taste. Serve, garnished with chopped coriander.

Freezing recommended

serves: **4**   preparation: **5** mins   cooking: **20** mins

POINTS PER SERVING

1

points per recipe
4

Grilled vegetable kebabs with a hot tomato glaze

V

- 1 aubergine, sliced into 2.5 cm (1-inch) thick rounds
- 1 red or yellow pepper, de-seeded and cut into chunks
- 2 courgettes, sliced thickly
- 4 teaspoons olive oil
- 2 tomatoes, skinned, de-seeded and chopped finely
- 1 shallot, chopped finely
- 4 teaspoons horseradish sauce
- salt and freshly ground black pepper

1 Cut the aubergine slices into quarters.

2 Preheat the grill to medium-high. Remove the rack and line the tray with foil. Thread the aubergine, pepper and courgettes on to 4 small skewers. Brush with the oil and season with salt and pepper. Grill for 15–20 minutes, turning and brushing with oil frequently, until the vegetables have softened and coloured.

3 Meanwhile, make the glaze by mixing together the tomatoes, shallot and horseradish sauce in a small bowl. Stir in any remaining oil and then use to brush over the vegetables for the last 5 minutes of grilling.

4 To serve, brush the kebabs with the remaining glaze and season to taste.

Freezing not recommended

Baked doughnuts

POINTS PER DOUGHNUT
1/2
points per recipe
10 1/2

V

1 Preheat the oven to Gas Mark 3/160°C/fan oven 140°C.

2 Place all the ingredients, except the extra sugar, cooking spray and cinnamon, in a large bowl and combine well to form a smooth batter.

3 Spray the doughnut baking tray(s) with the low-fat cooking spray. Half fill each doughnut mould with the batter mixture. (Specially shaped, moulded trays are available from good cookshops. Be careful not to overfill them otherwise the cooked doughnuts will not have any holes!)

4 Cook for 10–15 minutes, until risen and firm to the touch. (The bottom of the doughnuts brown faster than the tops!)

5 Meanwhile, on a small plate, mix together the dipping sugar and the cinnamon. Remove the cooked doughnuts from the tray one at a time, and dip the bottom of each into the sugar and cinnamon mixture, then leave to cool on a wire rack.

Freezing recommended

- **75 g (2 3/4 oz) plain flour**
- **1 teaspoon baking powder**
- **1 egg, beaten**
- **1 teaspoon corn oil**
- **1/2 teaspoon vanilla extract**
- **75 g (2 3/4 oz) caster sugar, plus 2 teaspoons for dipping**
- **4 tablespoons skimmed milk**
- **1/2 teaspoon salt**
- **low-fat cooking spray**
- **1/4 teaspoon ground cinnamon**

makes: **10**   preparation: **10** mins   cooking: **20** mins

POINTS PER COOKIE

1

points per recipe
9

- **50 g (1¾ oz) half-fat butter**
- **25 g (1 oz) caster sugar**
- **75 g (2¾ oz) plain flour**
- **½ teaspoon vanilla or almond essence**

Cookies

V

1 Preheat the oven to Gas Mark 4/180°C/fan oven 160°C.

2 Cream together the half-fat butter and sugar. Sift in the flour and add the vanilla or almond essence and mix until it all comes together as a firm dough. (If you have the time, chill the dough for 30 minutes before continuing.)

3 Divide the dough into 10 portions and roll each one into a ball.

4 Place on a non-stick baking tray and flatten them to a cookie size and shape.

5 Bake for 15–20 minutes, until pale gold. Leave to cool on the baking tray for 5 minutes and then transfer to a cooling rack.

Freezing not recommended

Apple drop scones

V

POINTS PER SCONE

1

points per recipe
21

1 Put the flour, cereal, apple, salt and sugar into a large bowl. Add the egg and milk and beat well until all the ingredients are thoroughly combined. Cover and allow to stand for 15 minutes.

2 Heat a large, heavy-based frying-pan or griddle until hot. Add a little oil, then drop tablespoons of the mixture into the hot pan. Cook until bubbles appear on the surface, then flip over to cook the other side.

3 Transfer the cooked drop scones on to kitchen paper to cool slightly. Cook the remaining batter in the same way until it is all used. Serve each scone with ¹/₂ teaspoon of very low-fat spread and a teaspoon of the strawberry jam.

Freezing not recommended

- **100 g (3¹/₂ oz) self-raising flour**
- **50 g (1³/₄ oz) Jordans Original Crunchy Cereal (Raisins and Almonds)**
- **1 dessert apple, peeled, cored and grated finely**
- **a pinch of salt**
- **25 g (1 oz) golden caster sugar**
- **1 large egg**
- **150 ml (¹/₄ pint) skimmed milk**
- **2 teaspoons vegetable oil**
- **9 teaspoons very low-fat spread (e.g. Flora Diet)**
- **18 teaspoons reduced-sugar strawberry jam**

makes: **24**   preparation: **15** mins   cooking: **15** mins

POINTS PER WEDGE
1
points per recipe
21

- **225 g (8 oz) demerara sugar**
- **½ tablespoon golden syrup**
- **25 g (1 oz) butter**
- **2 teaspoons lemon juice**
- **4 dessert apples, cored, each cut into 6 wedges**

Toffee apple wedges

V

1 Line two baking trays with non-stick parchment.

2 Place the sugar, syrup, butter, lemon juice and 5 tablespoons of water in a heavy-based saucepan and stir over a gentle heat until the sugar has dissolved.

3 Increase the heat and boil, without stirring, for 5 minutes or until half a teaspoon of the mixture becomes hard and brittle when dropped into a bowl of cold water. (Remove the pan from the heat before testing.)

4 Using long-handled tongs, place half the apple wedges in the pan of toffee, turning to make sure they are well coated. Remove, allowing the excess toffee to drip away. Spread the apples out on the non-stick parchment. Repeat with the remaining wedges.

5 Leave to set in a cool dry place until serving. If desired, wrap each wedge in a piece of cellophane.

Freezing not recommended

2 points
and under

Ham, leek and potato soup

Glazed sausage kebabs

Tuna cakes with spring onion salsa

Spicy turkey marrow

Mixed bean chilli

Low-fat sticky gingerbread

Orange semolina puddings

Lemon madeleines

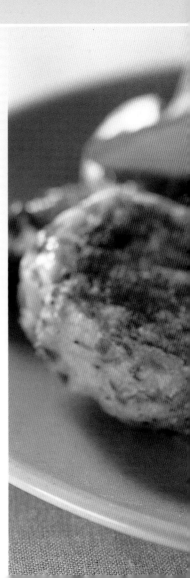

points per recipe
6

Ham, leek and potato soup

- **2 leeks, sliced finely**
- **100 g (3½ oz) potatoes, peeled and sliced finely**
- **600 ml (1 pint) hot vegetable stock**
- **1 tablespoon cornflour**
- **200 ml (7 fl oz) semi-skimmed milk**
- **2 tablespoons chopped fresh parsley (or 2 teaspoons dried)**
- **150 g (5½ oz) wafer-thin smoked ham, cut into pieces**
- **2 teaspoons Dijon or wholegrain mustard**
- **salt and freshly ground black pepper**

1 Put the leeks and potatoes into a saucepan with the hot stock. Cover and simmer for 10 minutes.

2 In a small bowl, blend the cornflour with the milk then stir in the parsley. Add to the potatoes and leeks, stirring until the mixture thickens slightly. Cover and simmer for a further 10 minutes.

3 Add the ham and the mustard to the saucepan. Season to taste. Heat gently for another minute or two then serve.

Freezing recommended

Glazed sausage kebabs

1 Make the glaze by gently heating all the glaze ingredients together in a small pan, stirring to mix for a couple of minutes.

2 Meanwhile, heat the grill to medium. Thread alternate pieces of sausage, courgette, tomato, apple and onion on to 8 small skewers.

3 Grill the kebabs for 12–15 minutes, brushing them with the glaze and turning them regularly. Mix any pan juices with left over glaze and drizzle it over the kebabs to serve.

Freezing not recommended

points per recipe
11

- **8 × 95% fat-free sausages, each cut into thirds**
- **2 courgettes, sliced thickly**
- **8 small tomatoes, halved**
- **2 dessert apples, cored, and cut into eighths**
- **4 small onions, quartered**
  For the glaze
- **2 tablespoons mango chutney**
- **2 tablespoons orange juice**
- **1 tablespoon coarse-grain mustard**
- **1/2 teaspoon ground ginger**

Tuna cakes with spring onion salsa

1 Boil the potatoes in lightly salted water for 15–20 minutes, until tender.

2 While the potatoes are cooking, in a small bowl mix together all the salsa ingredients then leave to marinate.

3 When the potatoes are just cooked through, drain and mash them, then stir in the tuna, the remaining lemon juice and season to taste. Divide the mixture into eight and shape into small cakes.

4 Heat the oil in a large, non-stick frying-pan and fry the cakes for 3 minutes. Then gently turn them over and cook for a further 2 minutes.

5 Serve two tuna cakes per person with a helping of salsa.

Freezing not recommended

POINTS PER SERVING

2

points per recipe
8

- **400 g (14 oz) potatoes, peeled and diced**
- **185 g can tuna chunks in brine or spring water, drained and flaked roughly**
- **1 teaspoon lemon juice**
- **1 teaspoon olive oil**
- **salt and freshly ground black pepper**
  For the salsa
- **4 spring onions, chopped finely**
- **5 cm (2-inches) cucumber, seeds removed and flesh diced finely**
- **1 teaspoon lemon juice**

points per recipe
9

- **1 marrow, halved lengthways and de-seeded**
- **2 teaspoons vegetable oil**
- **1 onion, chopped**
- **1 carrot, grated**
- **1 red pepper, de-seeded and chopped**
- **2 garlic cloves, crushed**
- **1 tablespoon mild curry powder or mixed spice**
- **275 g (9½ oz) turkey mince**
- **2 tablespoons chopped fresh herbs (or 1 tablespoon dried herbs)**
- **1 tablespoon soy sauce**
- **1 chicken stock cube, dissolved in 150 ml (¼ pint) hot water**
- **2 tablespoons half-fat crème fraîche**
- **salt and freshly ground black pepper**

Spicy turkey marrow

1 Preheat the oven to Gas Mark 6/200°C/fan oven 180°F. Place the marrow in a large baking dish or roasting tin, cut sides facing up.

2 Heat the oil in a large saucepan, add the onion and sauté gently for 2–3 minutes. Add the carrot, red pepper and garlic and cook gently for another 3–4 minutes until softened. Stir in the curry powder or mixed spice and cook for 1 minute more.

3 Stir the turkey mince into the vegetables then add the herbs and soy sauce. Cook for 2–3 minutes over a medium-high heat, then add the chicken stock. Heat until boiling, then reduce the heat and simmer for about 10 minutes, uncovered, until the stock has been reduced by half. Season to taste with salt and pepper.

4 Remove from the heat and stir in the crème fraîche. Spoon the mixture into the hollowed-out marrow. Add about 150 ml (¼ pint) of cold water to the baking dish or tin around the marrow, then cover the dish with the foil and bake for 35–40 minutes, until the marrow is tender.

Freezing not recommended

Mixed bean chilli

V

POINTS PER SERVING

2

points per recipe
4

1 Heat the olive oil in a pan and cook the onion, garlic, carrot, peppers and mushrooms for 5 minutes.

2 Stir in the apple and chilli powder and cook for a further 2 minutes.

3 Stir in the tomatoes and mixed beans with their sauce. Cover and simmer for 20 minutes then remove the lid and cook for a further 10 minutes to reduce the liquid, increasing the heat if necessary.

4 Season to taste and serve hot, garnished with the chopped parsley.

Freezing recommended

- **1 teaspoon olive oil**
- **1 small onion, sliced**
- **1 garlic clove, crushed**
- **1 carrot, diced**
- **1/2 red pepper, de-seeded and diced**
- **1/2 green pepper, de-seeded and diced**
- **75 g (2 3/4 oz) button mushrooms, quartered**
- **1/2 cooking apple, cored, peeled and grated**
- **1/2 tablespoon mild chilli powder**
- **200 g can chopped tomatoes**
- **200 g (7 oz) canned mixed beans in spicy sauce**
- **salt and freshly ground black pepper**
- **1 tablespoon chopped fresh parsley, to garnish**

makes: **20** slices　　preparation: **15** mins + cooling　　cooking: **1¼–1½** hrs

POINTS PER SLICE
1½

points per recipe
30½

- **40 g (1½ oz) low-fat spread (e.g. St Ivel 'Gold')**
- **2 tablespoons marmalade**
- **100 g (3½ oz) golden syrup**
- **100 g (3½ oz) black treacle**
- **50 g (1¾ oz) soft brown sugar**
- **150 ml (¼ pint) skimmed milk**
- **low-fat cooking spray**
- **75 g (2¾ oz) wholemeal flour**
- **75 g (2¾ oz) self-raising flour**
- **1 teaspoon ground ginger**
- **1 teaspoon mixed spice**
- **¼ teaspoon bicarbonate of soda**
- **50 g (1¾ oz) porridge oats**
- **1 large egg**

Low-fat sticky gingerbread

V

1 Put the low-fat spread, marmalade, syrup, treacle and sugar into a large, heavy-based saucepan and heat until bubbling, stirring well. Simmer gently for a few minutes until the sugar has completely dissolved. Remove from the heat and cool, then stir in the milk.

2 Preheat the oven to Gas Mark 2/150°C/fan oven 130°C. Spray an 18 cm (7-inch) square, deep cake tin with the low-fat cooking spray and line the base and sides with non-stick baking parchment, cutting it to fit.

3 Put the flours, spices, bicarbonate of soda and the oats in a large bowl and stir well to mix.

4 When the mixture in the saucepan is cold, add the dry ingredients and the egg and beat until smooth. Pour this into the prepared tin.

5 Bake for 1¼–1½ hours until the cake has risen and is firm to the touch. Cool in the tin for ½ hour, then turn out on to a wire rack and leave to cool completely. Peel off the baking parchment, wrap the cake in clingfilm and leave for at least a day so that it becomes nice and sticky. The gingerbread will keep for about a week.

Freezing recommended

Orange semolina puddings

points per recipe
8½

V

1 Preheat the oven to Gas Mark 5/190°C/fan oven 170°C.

2 Put the semolina in a saucepan and stir in the milk. Bring to the boil, stirring constantly until thickened. Reduce the heat and cook gently for 2–3 minutes.

3 Remove from the heat, leave to cool for a few minutes then add sweetener to taste. Stir in the orange zest and egg yolks. Divide the mixture between four individual heatproof dishes or ramekins. Top with the orange segments.

4 Beat the egg whites in a grease-free bowl until they hold their shape. Whisk in the sugar then pile this on top of the desserts. Bake for 3–5 minutes until golden brown. Serve at once.

Freezing not recommended

- **25 g (1 oz) semolina**
- **450 ml (16 fl oz) skimmed milk**
- **powdered sweetener, to taste**
- **finely grated zest and segments of 1 large orange**
- **2 large eggs, separated**
- **1 tablespoon caster sugar**

makes: **24**   preparation + cooking: **30** mins + chilling

POINTS PER SERVING

2

points per serving
43

- **low-fat cooking spray**
- **125 g (4½ oz) caster sugar**
- **4 eggs**
- **finely grated zest of 2 lemons**
- **125 g (4½ oz) plain flour**
- **1 teaspoon baking powder**
- **1 pinch of salt**
- **100 g (3½ oz) butter, melted and cooled**
- **2 teaspoons icing sugar, to dust**

Lemon madeleines

1 Lightly spray two trays of madeleine moulds with the low-fat cooking spray.

2 In a large bowl, whisk together the caster sugar, eggs and lemon zest until pale, fluffy and thick enough to leave a trail when the whisk is lifted.

3 Sift in half the flour with the baking powder and the salt. Drizzle half the butter over and then carefully fold in using a metal spoon. Repeat with the remaining flour and butter. Cover and chill for 40 minutes.

4 Preheat the oven to Gas Mark 7/220°C/fan oven 200°C.

5 Fill the prepared moulds two-thirds full with the mixture and bake for 10 minutes until well risen, golden and springy to the touch. Carefully remove the madeleines from the moulds and transfer to a wire rack to cool. Dust with icing sugar before serving.

Freezing recommended

3 points
and under

Spicy pork casserole

Tomato and basil risotto

Spanish cod

Vegetable lasagne

Easy chicken casserole

Chocolate mousse

Apple and cinnamon flapjacks

Banana muffins

Grilled chocolate peaches

POINTS PER SERVING

2½

points per recipe
10½

- **500 g (1 lb 2 oz) lean boneless pork, cubed**
- **2 teaspoons sunflower oil**
- **1 onion, sliced**
- **1 red pepper, de-seeded and sliced**
- **1 large leek, sliced into 1 cm (½-inch) rounds**
- **1 large garlic clove, crushed**
- **1 teaspoon paprika**
- **1 teaspoon mild curry powder**
- **1 tablespoon plain flour**
- **200 g (7 oz) canned chopped tomatoes**
- **½ teaspoon sugar**
- **1 teaspoon grated orange or lemon zest (optional)**
- **1 bay leaf**
- **a handful of flat-leaf parsley, to garnish (optional)**
- **salt and freshly ground black pepper**

Spicy pork casserole

1 Heat a non-stick frying pan until hot then add the meat and dry-fry until brown. Remove the meat and add the oil to the pan together with the onion, red pepper, leek, garlic and 1–2 tablespoons water. Cover and cook gently for 5 minutes until softened.

2 Sprinkle in the spices and cook for 1 minute then stir in the flour and cook for 1 minute more .

3 Add the tomatoes, sugar, zest (if using), bay leaf, seasoning and about 300 ml (½ pint) water. Bring to the boil, stirring, then return the meat to the pan and mix it in. Cover and simmer for 45–60 minutes. For a thicker sauce, remove the lid 10–15 minutes before the end of the cooking time to allow the liquid to reduce. Garnish with parsley, if desired.

Freezing recommended

serves: **2**   preparation: **10** mins   cooking: **30** mins

points per recipe
6 1/2

Tomato and basil risotto

V

- low-fat cooking spray
- 40 g (1 1/2 oz) onion, chopped finely
- 1 garlic clove, crushed
- 100 g (3 1/2 oz) Arborio rice or risotto rice
- 300 ml (1/2 pint) tomato juice
- 250 ml (9 fl oz) vegetable stock
- 1 tablespoon sun-dried tomato purée
- 2 ripe tomatoes, skinned, de-seeded and diced
- 2 tablespoons very low-fat plain fromage frais
- 2 tablespoons torn fresh basil leaves, plus 4 whole leaves, to garnish
- salt and freshly ground black pepper

1 Spray a non-stick saucepan with the low-fat cooking spray. Add the onion and garlic and cook gently for 5 minutes until softened, but not coloured. Add the rice and cook for a further minute, stirring frequently. The rice will become opaque.

2 In a small saucepan, heat the tomato juice and stock to simmering point. Add a ladle of the liquid to the rice and stir continuously until all the liquid has been absorbed. Repeat, stirring after each addition of liquid, until all the liquid has been used. If the rice is still a little hard, add a couple of tablespoons of water and continue cooking until it becomes tender and creamy.

3 Stir in the tomato purée, fresh tomatoes, fromage frais and torn basil leaves. Season well and serve immediately, garnished with the remaining basil leaves.

Freezing not recommended

Spanish cod

1 Put the fish, wine and stock in a large frying-pan and poach for about 5 minutes or until the flesh becomes opaque.

2 Remove the fish, set aside and keep warm. Boil the cooking liquid, uncovered, until reduced by half.

3 Add the remaining ingredients and simmer for 2−3 minutes, to reduce further and thicken slightly.

4 Serve the fish with the sauce spooned over.

Freezing: not recommended

POINTS PER SERVING
3
points per recipe
3

- **150 g (5½ oz) chunky cod fillet**
- **50 ml (2 fl oz) white wine**
- **75 ml (3 fl oz) vegetable or fish stock**
- **25 g (1 oz) bottled pimientos, drained and chopped finely**
- **2 large pieces of sun-dried tomatoes, soaked in hot water for 15 minutes then drained and chopped finely**
- **½ teaspoon whole-grain mustard**
- **½ tablespoon finely chopped fresh parsley**

serves: **4**   preparation: **15** mins   cooking: **45** mins

points per recipe
13

- **1 onion, chopped**
- **1 courgette, sliced**
- **100 g (3¹/₂ oz) fine green beans, trimmed and chopped**
- **1 red pepper, de-seeded and chopped**
- **100 g (3¹/₂ oz) mushrooms, sliced**
- **400 g (14 oz) canned chopped tomatoes**
- **275 g jar of tomato pasta sauce with herbs**
- **125 g (4¹/₂ oz) lasagne sheets (about 6)**
- **150 g (5¹/₂ oz) low-fat plain yogurt**
- **1 egg**
- **50 g (1³/₄ oz) half-fat Cheddar cheese, grated**
- **salt and freshly ground black pepper**

Vegetable lasagne

V

1 Preheat the oven to Gas Mark 5/190°C/fan oven 170°C.

2 Put the onion, courgette, green beans and red pepper into a large saucepan with enough lightly salted boiling water to almost cover them, then simmer for about 5 minutes until just tender. Drain well, then add the mushrooms, tomatoes and pasta sauce to the pan and mix together well.

3 Spoon half the vegetable mixture into an oblong ovenproof lasagne dish and top with half the lasagne sheets. Spoon the rest of the vegetable mixture on top and cover with the remaining lasagne sheets.

4 Beat together the yogurt and egg. Season with salt and pepper and mix in half the cheese. Spread this mixture over the surface of the lasagne then sprinkle over the remaining cheese. Bake for 35–40 minutes until golden brown.

Freezing recommended

Easy chicken casserole

1 Preheat the oven to Gas Mark 4/180°C/fan oven 160°C.

2 Heat the vegetable oil in a large, flameproof casserole dish and sauté the leeks, celery, carrots, onion and parsnip for 3–4 minutes, until softened. Remove the vegetables from the casserole dish and set to one side.

3 Put the chicken in the casserole dish and cook until sealed on all sides. Return the vegetables to the dish and add the chicken stock, parsley and bay leaf. Season with salt and pepper.

4 Cover the casserole and cook in the oven for 1–1¼ hours.

5 Remove the casserole from the oven and discard the bay leaf. In a small bowl, blend the cornflour with a little cold water then add to the casserole, stirring to mix. Cover, return to the oven and cook for 5 minutes more.

6 Serve the casserole on warmed serving plates.

Freezing recommended

POINTS PER SERVING

3

points per recipe
11½

- **1 tablespoon vegetable oil**
- **2 leeks, sliced into rounds**
- **2 celery sticks, chopped**
- **2 carrots, sliced**
- **1 onion, chopped**
- **1 parsnip, chopped**
- **450 g (1 lb) skinless, boneless chicken, cut into large chunks**
- **600 ml (1 pint) chicken stock**
- **1 tablespoon chopped fresh parsley**
- **1 bay leaf**
- **1 tablespoon cornflour**
- **salt and freshly ground black pepper**

Chocolate mousse

POINTS PER SERVING

2½

points per recipe
13½

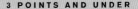

1 Put the chocolate in a large, heatproof bowl.

2 Place the bowl over a saucepan of gently simmering water and heat the chocolate until melted. (Be careful not to allow any water into the bowl.) Remove the bowl from the heat and set to one side.

3 In a large grease-free bowl, and using scrupulously clean beaters, whisk the egg whites until stiff.

4 Using a large metal spoon, fold one tablespoon of the egg white through the warm chocolate to 'loosen' it, then fold in the remaining egg white. Fold very gently to avoid losing too much air.

5 Divide the mixture between six small serving glasses or dishes, allowing enough space to finish off with the raspberries. Refrigerate until set.

6 Serve, topped with the raspberries, decorated with mint leaves and a dusting of icing sugar.

Freezing not recommended

- **100 g (3½ oz) good quality dark chocolate (70% cocoa solids), broken into pieces**
- **3 egg whites**
  To decorate
- **175 g (6 oz) raspberries**
- **mint leaves**
- **1 teaspoon icing sugar, to dust**

makes: **12** preparation: **10** mins cooking: **15** mins

POINTS PER FLAPJACK
2½

points per recipe
28

- **100 g (3½ oz) low-fat spread (e.g. St Ivel 'Gold')**
- **75 g (2¾ oz) dark muscovado sugar**
- **2 tablespoons golden syrup**
- **175 g (6 oz) porridge oats**
- **1 teaspoon ground cinnamon**
- **75 g (2¾ oz) dried apple chunks, chopped into bite-size pieces**
- **25 g (1 oz) raisins or currants**

Apple and cinnamon flapjacks

Ⓥ

1 Preheat the oven to Gas Mark 5/190°C/fan oven 170°C. Line an 18 cm (7-inch) shallow, square tin with greaseproof baking paper.

2 Put the low-fat spread, sugar and syrup in a large, heavy-based saucepan and heat gently, stirring occasionally, until melted and well blended.

3 Mix in the oats, cinnamon, apple pieces and raisins or currants.

4 Spread the mixture into the prepared tin then bake for 15 minutes. Leave to cool in the tin before cutting into 12 squares. Once completely cold, remove from the tin and store in an airtight container for up to a week.

Freezing recommended

Banana muffins

POINTS PER MUFFIN

2½

points per recipe
32

V

1 Preheat the oven to Gas Mark 5/190°C/fan oven 170°C.
Put 12 paper cases in suitable muffin tins.

2 Sift together the flour, baking powder, bicarbonate of soda
and salt.

3 In another bowl, beat together the egg, 5 teaspoons of water,
the sugar and banana purée.

4 Add the corn oil to the beaten ingredients and stir well.

5 Quickly combine the two sets of ingredients and mix just enough
to combine – it should have a lumpy consistency.

6 Spoon the mixture into the paper cases and bake for 20–25
minutes, until firm and springy, then remove from the oven and
leave to cool on a rack.

Freezing recommended

- **250 g (9 oz) plain flour**
- **1 teaspoon baking powder**
- **1 teaspoon bicarbonate
  of soda**
- **½ teaspoon salt**
- **1 egg, beaten**
- **80 g (3 oz) soft brown
  sugar**
- **3 well-ripened bananas,
  peeled and mashed to
  a purée**
- **4 tablespoons corn oil**

serves: **4**   preparation + cooking: **10** mins

points per recipe
9

- **2 fresh ripe peaches, halved and stoned**
- **50 g (1¾ oz) plain chocolate (70% cocoa solids), chopped into pieces**
- **125 g (4½ oz) 0% fat Greek-style yogurt**
- **4 teaspoons light or dark soft brown sugar**

Grilled chocolate peaches

V

1 Preheat the grill to high. Place the peach halves in four ramekin dishes, cut side up.

2 Evenly divide the chocolate and place inside the hollow in each peach. Spoon the yogurt over so that the peach flesh is completely covered. Evenly sprinkle the sugar over the surface.

3 Grill for 4 – 5 minutes, until the sugar has dissolved and the surface is bubbling. Serve immediately.

Freezing not recommended

4 points
and under

Gnocchi with quick tomato sauce

Eastern salmon

Minted lamb casserole

Steak fajita

Turkey tomato pasta

Savoury vegetable crumble

Ginger puddings

Banana bread

Apple and walnut pie

POINTS PER SERVING

4

points per recipe
8

- **350 g (12 oz) packet of fresh, chilled gnocchi**
- **1 tablespoon parmesan cheese, grated**
- **torn basil leaves, to garnish**
  For the tomato sauce
- **1 small onion, chopped finely**
- **½ tablespoon tomato purée**
- **400 g (14 oz) canned, chopped tomatoes with chilli**
- **150 ml (¼ pint) vegetable stock**
- **½ teaspoon sugar**
- **salt and freshly ground black pepper**

Gnocchi with quick tomato sauce

V

1 Place all the ingredients for the tomato sauce in a saucepan. Bring to the boil and simmer vigorously, uncovered, for about 20 minutes until the liquid has been reduced to a thick sauce. Season to taste.

2 Meanwhile, cook the gnocchi according to the pack instructions. Preheat the grill to high.

3 Spoon a little sauce in the base of two shallow, flameproof bowls. Add the drained gnocchi then pour the remaining sauce over. Sprinkle with the cheese. Grill for 2 minutes until the cheese turns golden brown.

4 Scatter the basil leaves over and serve immediately.

Freezing recommended for the sauce only

Eastern salmon

1 Preheat the oven to Gas Mark 6/200°C/fan oven 180°C.

2 Mix together the soy sauce, honey and Chinese five spice powder in a shallow, ovenproof dish, just big enough to take the fillets.

3 Roll the salmon in the mixture so that all the sides are coated. Place them skin side down in the dish.

4 Bake in the oven for 20 minutes until the fish is cooked.

Freezing not recommended

points per recipe
7 1/2

- **1 tablespoon soy sauce**
- **1/2 teaspoon clear honey**
- **1/2 teaspoon Chinese five spice powder**
- **2 × 125 g (4 1/2 oz) salmon fillets**

serves: **4**   preparation: **10** mins   cooking: **1¾** hrs

POINTS PER SERVING

3½

points per recipe
13

- **400 g (14 oz) lean diced lamb**
- **4 carrots, diced**
- **1 leek, sliced into rounds**
- **2 celery sticks, chopped**
- **4 teaspoons gravy granules**
- **500 ml (18 fl oz) hot vegetable or lamb stock**
- **1 tablespoon mint sauce**

Minted lamb casserole

1 Preheat the oven to Gas Mark 3/160°C/fan oven 140°C.

2 Put the lamb and vegetables into a casserole dish.

3 Add the gravy granules to the hot stock then stir in the mint sauce. Pour this into the casserole dish over the lamb and vegetables. Cover and cook for 1½ hours.

4 Uncover, stir and cook for a further 15 minutes before serving.

Freezing recommended

Steak fajita

1 Put the steak in a bowl with the lime juice, garlic and oil. Cover and refrigerate for about 1 hour.

2 Remove the steak from the marinade with a slotted spoon and place it in a hot wok or large frying-pan. Stir-fry the meat for 1–2 minutes or until cooked to taste, then remove it and set to one side. Add the vegetables to the pan with the remaining marinade juices and stir-fry for 2–3 minutes.

3 Meanwhile, warm the tortilla by microwaving on high for 10–15 seconds, or heat in an oven according to the pack instructions.

4 Return the meat to the pan with the vegetables, stir well and season with salt and pepper, then wrap the stir-fry in the warmed tortilla, and serve immediately.

Freezing not recommended

POINTS PER SERVING

4

points per recipe
4

- **50 g (1¾ oz) good quality steak, cut into thin strips**
- **juice of ½ lime**
- **1 small garlic clove, crushed**
- **½ teaspoon olive oil**
- **½ green or red pepper, de-seeded and cut into strips**
- **1 mushroom, sliced**
- **1 small onion, sliced**
- **1 tomato, sliced**
- **1 medium soft flour tortilla**
- **salt and freshly ground black pepper**

serves: **4**   preparation: **10** mins   cooking: **20** mins

POINTS PER SERVING
3 1/2

points per recipe
14 1/2

- **2 teaspoons olive oil**
- **a bunch of spring onions, sliced finely**
- **1 garlic clove, crushed**
- **1 green pepper, de-seeded and chopped**
- **50 g (1 3/4 oz) sun-dried tomatoes in olive oil, rinsed and sliced**
- **200 ml (7 fl oz) tomato juice or 400 g (14 oz) canned chopped tomatoes**
- **1 tablespoon dried oregano or Italian mixed dried herbs**
- **175 g (6 oz) pasta shapes (e.g. shells)**
- **150 g (5 1/2 oz) pack of turkey rashers**
- **salt and freshly ground black pepper**
- **oregano or basil leaves, to garnish (optional)**

Turkey tomato pasta

1 Heat the oil in a large saucepan and sauté the spring onions and garlic for about 2 minutes, or until soft. Add the green pepper and cook, stirring, for 2 minutes more.

2 Add the tomato products and the dried herbs. Heat until bubbling, then turn the heat to low and simmer, uncovered, for 10 minutes.

3 Meanwhile, cook the pasta in a large pan of boiling, lightly salted water for 8–10 minutes, until just tender.

4 At the same time, grill the turkey rashers for 1 1/2 minutes on each side, then cut into small pieces.

5 Drain the pasta well then add it to the sauce with three-quarters of the chopped turkey pieces. Season to taste. Divide between four warmed plates and garnish with oregano or basil leaves, if using, and the reserved turkey pieces. Sprinkle with black pepper and serve immediately.

Freezing not recommended

serves: **4**   preparation: **25** mins   cooking: **40** mins

points per recipe
15½

Savoury vegetable crumble

V

1 Preheat the oven to Gas Mark 5/190°C/fan oven 170°C.

2 Heat the oil and soy sauce in a pan and add the leeks, carrots, mushrooms, corn and peas. Cover and cook over a low heat for 5 minutes, stirring half-way through.

3 Stir in the soup, season to taste and heat through. Transfer to a shallow, ovenproof dish.

4 Sift the flour into a mixing bowl and stir in the oats. Rub in the low-fat spread using your fingertips then stir in the cheese. Sprinkle this over the vegetable mixture then bake for 30 minutes, until the topping is golden and crunchy. Serve hot.

Freezing recommended

- **1 teaspoon vegetable oil**
- **1 tablespoon soy sauce**
- **2 leeks, sliced**
- **2 carrots, diced**
- **225 g (8 oz) button mushrooms, quartered**
- **175 g (6 oz) baby corn, halved lengthways**
- **100 g (3½ oz) frozen peas**
- **295 g can of Weight Watchers from Heinz Vegetable Soup**
- **salt and freshly ground black pepper**
  For the crumble
- **100 g (3½ oz) plain flour**
- **25 g (1 oz) rolled oats**
- **50 g (1¾ oz) low-fat spread**
- **50 g (1¾ oz) reduced-fat Red Leicester cheese, grated**

Ginger puddings

V

POINTS PER SERVING
3½
points per recipe
14½

1 Preheat the oven to Gas Mark 5/190°C/fan oven 170°C. Spray 4 × 150 ml (¼ pint) pudding basins (tin, glass or foil) with the low-fat cooking spray.

2 Sift all the dry ingredients, except the brown sugar, into a bowl. Add the brown sugar then whisk in the rest of the ingredients.

3 Divide between the prepared pudding basins and place them on a baking tray. Bake in the oven for 25 – 30 minutes, until firm to the touch.

4 Cool in the basins for 5 minutes before loosening with a knife and turning out on to serving plates.

Freezing recommended

- **low-fat cooking spray**
- **80 g (3 oz) self-raising flour**
- **1 teaspoon ground ginger**
- **¼ teaspoon ground cinnamon**
- **¼ teaspoon baking powder**
- **¼ teaspoon bicarbonate of soda**
- **40 g (1½ oz) soft brown sugar**
- **1 egg, beaten**
- **8 teaspoons corn oil**
- **2 teaspoons golden syrup**

Banana bread

points per slice

3½

points per recipe
43

(v)

1 Preheat the oven to Gas Mark 4/180°C/fan oven 160°C. Spray a 450 g (1 lb) loaf tin with the low-fat cooking spray.

2 In a large bowl, sieve the flour and bicarbonate of soda together.

3 In another bowl, cream the butter, sugar and honey or extra tablespoon of sugar, if using, until light and fluffy.

4 Add the eggs gradually, beating all the time.

5 Gently stir the flour into the creamed mixture.

6 Stir in the mashed bananas and sultanas, if using. Spoon into the prepared tin and bake for about an hour or until just firm.

7 Turn out and cool on a rack. Wrap in cling film and store in a tin. This bread is best kept for a day before eating.

Freezing recommended

- **low-fat cooking spray**
- **200 g (7 oz) self-raising flour**
- **¼ teaspoon bicarbonate of soda**
- **75 g (2¾ oz) butter**
- **75 g (2¾ oz) sugar**
- **1 tablespoon honey, or an extra tablespoon sugar (optional)**
- **2 eggs, beaten**
- **2 ripe bananas, mashed**
- **100 g (3½ oz) sultanas (optional)**

serves: **8**   preparation: **15 mins**   cooking: **1 hr**

points per recipe
33½

- **25 g (1 oz) walnut pieces, toasted**
- **25 g (1 oz) butter**
- **50 g (1¾ oz) caster sugar**
- **1 egg**
- **grated rind and juice of 1 small lemon**
- **25 g (1 oz) self-raising flour**
- **1 teaspoon ground cinnamon**
- **8 crisp eating apples (e.g. Cox)**
- **1 tablespoon sultanas**
- **270 g pack filo pastry sheets**
- **low-fat cooking spray**
- **1 teaspoon icing sugar, sieved, to dust**

Apple and walnut pie

Ⓥ

1 Preheat the oven to Gas Mark 5/190°C/fan oven 170°C. Process the nuts in a food processor until chopped finely.

2 In a small bowl, cream together the butter and 40 g (1½ oz) of the sugar.

3 Whisk in the egg, then the lemon rind, flour and ½ teaspoon of the cinnamon. Finally mix in the nuts.

4 Peel, core and slice the apples, put in a large bowl and toss with the lemon juice, sultanas and the remaining sugar and cinnamon.

5 Line a 23 cm (9-inch) metal flan dish with three-quarters of the pastry. Use the cooking spray to spray the part of each sheet that will form the base of the pie. Allow the unsprayed edges to overhang.

6 Spread the nut mixture over the base then top with apples. Gather up the overhanging pastry, scrunching up the sheets like paper. Scrunch up the remaining pastry and use to completely conceal the apple filling.

7 Lightly spray the top of the pie with the cooking spray. Bake for 50–60 minutes. Cover with foil if the pastry starts to brown too much.

8 Serve warm, dusted with the sieved icing sugar.

Freezing recommended

5 points
and under

Seafood paella

Moroccan chicken tagine

Italian meatballs

Pasta primavera

French-style sausage casserole

Baked strawberry alaskas

Tropical fruit crumble

Cherry cheesecake

Chocolate bread pudding with luscious

   chocolate sauce

serves: **4**   preparation: **15** mins   cooking: **25** mins

POINTS PER SERVING

4 1/2

points per recipe
18 1/2

- 1 teaspoon olive oil
- 1 small onion, chopped finely
- 1 garlic clove, crushed
- large pinch of saffron strands
- 1 red pepper, de-seeded and diced
- 225 g (8 oz) risotto rice
- 850 ml (1 1/2 pints) fish or vegetable stock
- 125 g (4 1/2 oz) frozen peas
- 225 g (8 oz) skinless cod fillet, cut into bite-size pieces
- 2 tablespoons fresh chopped parsley
- 125 g (4 1/2 oz) peeled prawns, plus four still in their shells
- salt and freshly ground black pepper

Seafood paella

1 Heat the oil in a frying-pan and add the onion and garlic. Cook over a low heat, stirring, until the onion has softened but not browned.

2 Place the saffron in a small dish and cover with 2 tablespoons of boiling water, leave to stand so that the saffron infuses and colours the water bright yellow.

3 Add the red pepper and rice to the pan together with the saffron, its soaking liquid and the stock. Bring to the boil and simmer, uncovered, for 15 minutes, until most of the liquid has been absorbed.

4 Add the peas and cod pieces then continue cooking for 5 minutes. Toss in the parsley and the peeled prawns, season to taste then cook for a further 2–3 minutes until piping hot. Serve with the unshelled prawns placed on top of the paella.

Freezing not recommended

Moroccan chicken tagine

points per recipe
17½

1 Put the chicken in a large saucepan with the onions and cinnamon sticks. Sprinkle with the ginger and coriander, then add salt to taste. Cover with water and simmer gently, covered, for 1 hour.

2 Add the apricots and the honey then cook for a further 30 minutes, uncovered, until the sauce has reduced considerably. Season to taste, and serve with half a tablespoon of crème fraîche and the chopped coriander, if using, sprinkled over the top.

Freezing not recommended

- **4 × 175 g (6 oz) skinless, boneless chicken breasts**
- **2 onions, chopped finely**
- **2 cinnamon sticks**
- **½ teaspoon ground ginger**
- **½ teaspoon ground coriander**
- **150 g (5½ oz) ready-to-eat apricots, chopped**
- **1 tablespoon honey**
- **2 tablespoons half-fat crème fraîche**
- **2 tablespoons chopped fresh coriander (optional)**
- **salt and freshly ground black pepper**

serves: **4**   preparation: **20** mins   cooking: **40** mins

POINTS PER SERVING
4½
points per recipe
17½

- **350 g (12 oz) lean lamb mince**
- **25 g (1 oz) fresh breadcrumbs**
- **1 small onion, chopped finely**
- **1 garlic clove, crushed**
- **1 teaspoon dried oregano**
- **1 teaspoon dried basil**
- **1 egg, beaten**
- **400 g (14 oz) canned chopped tomatoes**
- **300 ml (½ pint) tomato juice**
- **1 lamb or beef stock cube**
- **salt and freshly ground black pepper**
- **2 tablespoons torn fresh basil leaves, to garnish**

Italian meatballs

1 Place the mince in a mixing bowl with the breadcrumbs, onion, garlic, dried herbs, egg and seasoning. Mix together thoroughly then shape the mixture into 16 small balls.

2 Heat a large, non-stick frying-pan and dry-fry the meatballs for 2–3 minutes to lightly brown and seal on all sides. Add the chopped tomatoes and tomato juice to the pan and crumble in the stock cube.

3 Bring to the boil, stirring, then cover. Reduce the heat and simmer for 30 minutes. Place four meatballs on to each of the four plates and divide the sauce between them. Scatter with the fresh basil and serve.

Freezing recommended

serves: **2**   preparation: **5** mins   cooking: **10** mins

POINTS PER SERVING
4¹/₂
points per recipe
9¹/₂

- 150 g (5¹/₂ oz) pasta (e.g. farfalle or penne)
- low-fat cooking spray
- 100 g (3¹/₂ oz) asparagus, cut into 2.5 cm (1-inch) lengths
- 150 g (5¹/₂ oz) sugar snap peas
- 150 g (5¹/₂ oz) baby carrots, trimmed and cut in half lengthways
- 1 tablespoon dry white wine
- 75 g (2³/₄ oz) very low-fat soft cheese (e.g. Philadelphia Extra Light)
- ¹/₂ tablespoon chopped fresh dill
- salt and freshly ground black pepper

Pasta primavera

V

1 Cook the pasta according to the pack instructions.

2 Meanwhile, spray a large saucepan or wok with the low-fat cooking spray and put on a medium heat. Add all the vegetables and stir-fry for 4–6 minutes, adding the white wine towards the end of the cooking time.

3 Add the soft cheese and gently stir in. Drain the pasta, reserving 2 tablespoons of the cooking liquid and add this and the pasta to the vegetable mixture. Add the chopped dill, season to taste, stir well and serve immediately.

Freezing not recommended

French-style sausage casserole

POINTS PER SERVING

5

points per recipe
20

1 Preheat the oven to Gas Mark 5/190°C/fan oven 170°C.

2 Put the sausages on a baking tray and place in the preheated oven for 8–10 minutes.

3 Spray a non-stick frying pan with the low-fat cooking spray and gently fry the garlic and onion until they start to brown.

4 Meanwhile, using the gravy granules and boiling water, make 250 ml (9 fl oz) of gravy then add the vinegar, mustard and the ale, stirring well to mix.

5 Transfer the onion and garlic mixture to a casserole dish and top with the part-baked sausages. Pour the gravy over them.

6 Reduce the oven temperature to Gas Mark 3/160°C/fan oven 140°C. Cover the casserole and cook for ¾ hour.

7 Remove the cover, baste the sausages with the gravy from the bottom of the dish and cook for 15 minutes more.

Freezing recommended

- **450 g (1 lb) pack of extra-lean sausages**
- **low-fat cooking spray**
- **1 garlic clove, crushed**
- **1 onion, chopped finely**
- **4 teaspoons gravy granules**
- **1 teaspoon white wine vinegar**
- **2 teaspoons whole-grain mustard**
- **200 ml (7 fl oz) brown ale**

serves: **4**   preparation + cooking: **20** mins

POINTS PER SERVING

4 1/2

points per recipe
17 1/2

- **4 × 25 g (1 oz) slices of jam Swiss Roll**
- **1 ripe peach or nectarine, skinned and stoned**
- **2 tablespoons sherry**
- **250 g (9 oz) strawberries, sliced thinly, reserving 4 whole strawberries to garnish**
- **1 egg white**
- **50 g (1 3/4 oz) caster sugar**
- **4 × 60 g (2 oz) scoops of Weight Watchers from Heinz Vanilla Iced Dessert**

Baked strawberry alaskas

V

1 Preheat the grill to high. Place the Swiss Roll slices in the bottom of four small ramekin dishes.

2 Mash or liquidise the peach or nectarine with the sherry. Spoon the purée over the sponge bases and top with the sliced strawberries.

3 Make a meringue mixture by whisking the egg white in a scrupulously clean bowl until stiff. Then whisk in the sugar, a little at a time, until the meringue becomes glossy.

4 Spoon a scoop of the iced dessert on top of the sliced strawberries, then swirl the meringue on top. Make sure that the meringue forms a seal, without gaps, around the edge of each ramekin dish to insulate the Iced Dessert from the heat.

5 Quickly heat under a hot grill until the meringue is tinged golden brown. Top each with a whole strawberry and serve immediately.

Freezing not recommended

Tropical fruit crumble

ⓥ

1 Preheat the oven to Gas Mark 5/190°C/fan oven 170°C. Lightly spray a deep 15 cm (6-inch) round, ovenproof dish with the low-fat cooking spray.

2 Layer the bananas and the pineapple with the juice and rum in the dish.

3 Mix the crumble with the muesli and spread this mixture over the fruit.

4 Bake for 30–35 minutes until golden brown. Serve hot or cold.

- **low-fat cooking spray**
- **2 bananas, sliced thinly**
- **225 g (8 oz) canned pineapple rings in fruit juice, cut into pieces, juice reserved**
- **30 ml (1 fl oz) white, dark or spiced rum**
- **140 g (5 oz) packet crumble mix**
- **50 g (1¾ oz) unsweetened wholewheat muesli with dried fruit**

Cherry cheesecake

1 Line an 18 cm (7-inch) loose-bottomed cake tin with greaseproof paper.

2 In a small pan, gently melt the low-fat spread then add the crushed biscuits.

3 Mix well then press into the base of the cake tin using your fingers. Chill.

4 Mix the reserved cherry juice, lemon juice and cornflour in a small pan and heat, stirring continuously, until thickened. Add sweetener to taste then set aside to cool. Chill in the refrigerator before use.

5 Just before serving, mix the low-fat soft cheese with the fromage frais then beat in the icing sugar.

6 Spread the cheese mixture over the chilled biscuit base and top with the cherries. Pour over the chilled sauce to serve.

Freezing not recommended

POINTS PER SERVING
4$\frac{1}{2}$
points per recipe
36$\frac{1}{2}$

- **75 g (2$\frac{3}{4}$ oz) low-fat spread (e.g. St Ivel 'Gold')**
- **225 g (8 oz) reduced-fat digestive biscuits, crushed**
- **425 g (15 oz) canned black cherries, drained and juice reserved**
- **1 teaspoon lemon juice**
- **2 teaspoons cornflour**
- **granulated sweetener, to taste**
- **125 g (4$\frac{1}{2}$ oz) low-fat soft cheese**
- **100 g (3$\frac{1}{2}$ oz) low-fat plain fromage frais**
- **25 g (1 oz) icing sugar, sieved**

serves: **4**   preparation: **20** mins + soaking: **1–2** hrs   cooking: **40** mins

POINTS PER SERVING
5
points per recipe
19½

- ½ teaspoon polyunsaturated margarine
- 6 slices reduced-calorie white bread, crusts removed and cut into squares
- 600 ml (1 pint) skimmed milk
- 2 tablespoons unsweetened cocoa powder
- 2 eggs
- 25 g (1 oz) dark or light muscovado sugar
- 1 teaspoon vanilla essence
- 1 teaspoon icing sugar, for dusting
  For the sauce
- 25 g (1 oz) plain chocolate (70% cocoa solids), broken into pieces
- 1 tablespoon unsweetened cocoa powder
- 150 ml (¼ pint) skimmed milk
- 1 tablespoon cornflour
- powdered sweetener, to taste

Chocolate bread pudding with luscious chocolate sauce

V

1 Grease a 20 cm (8-inch) square baking dish with the margarine. Layer the bread squares in the baking dish.

2 In a small pan, gently heat the milk and cocoa powder, stirring occasionally, until lukewarm.

3 In a clean bowl, whisk the eggs, sugar and vanilla essence together then add the warm milk mixture and beat well. Strain into the baking dish, making sure that all the bread is covered. Cover and chill for 1–2 hours.

4 Preheat the oven to Gas Mark 4/180°C/fan oven 160°C. Bake the pudding for about 35–40 minutes or until set. Remove from the oven and set aside for 5 minutes.

5 While it is cooling, make the sauce. Put the chocolate, cocoa powder, milk and cornflour in a saucepan. Heat gently, stirring until smooth and blended. Add sweetener to taste.

6 Dust the pudding with icing sugar and serve with the hot sauce.

Freezing not recommended

alaskas, baked strawberry 58

apples: apple and cinnamon

  flapjacks 36

  apple and walnut pie 50

  apple drop scones 15

  toffee apple wedges 16

baked doughnuts 13

baked strawberry alaskas 58

bananas: banana bread 49

  banana muffins 37

bean chilli, mixed 23

bread pudding, chocolate, with

  luscious chocolate sauce 62

butternut squash soup 7

casseroles: easy chicken

  casserole 33

  French-style sausage

    casserole 57

  minted lamb casserole 42

  spicy pork casserole 28

cheesecake, cherry 61

chicken: easy chicken casserole 33

  Moroccan chicken tagine 53

chilli, mixed bean 23

chocolate: chocolate bread

  pudding with luscious

    chocolate sauce 62

  chocolate mousse 35

  grilled chocolate peaches 38

cod, Spanish 31

cookies 14

crumble: savoury vegetable

  crumble 46

  tropical fruit crumble 59

curry, mushroom 8

doughnuts, baked 13

Eastern salmon 41

easy chicken casserole 33

fajita, steak 43

flapjacks, apple and cinnamon 36

French-style sausage casserole 57

fruit crumble, tropical 59

ginger puddings 47

gingerbread, low-fat sticky 24

glazed sausage kebabs 19

gnocchi with quick tomato sauce 40

grilled chocolate peaches 38

grilled vegetable kebabs with a

  hot tomato glaze 12

ham, leek and potato soup 18

Italian meatballs 54

kebabs: grilled vegetable kebabs

  with a hot tomato glaze 12

  glazed sausage kebabs 19

lamb casserole, minted 42

lasagne, vegetable 32

lemon madeleines 26

low-fat sticky gingerbread 24

madeleines, lemon 26

marrow, spicy turkey 22

meatballs, Italian 54

minted lamb casserole 42

mixed bean chilli 23

Moroccan chicken tagine 53

Moroccan vegetable stew   10

mousse, chocolate   35

muffins, banana   37

mushroom curry   8

orange semolina puddings   25

oven-roasted tomato tartlets   9

paella, seafood   52

pasta: pasta primavera   56

   turkey tomato pasta   44

   vegetable lasagne   32

peaches, grilled chocolate   38

pie, apple and walnut   50

pork casserole, spicy   28

potato soup; ham, leek and   18

puddings: ginger puddings   47

   orange semolina puddings   25

risotto, tomato and basil   30

salmon, Eastern   41

sausage casserole, French-style 57

sausage kebabs, glazed   19

savoury vegetable crumble   46

scones, apple drop   15

seafood paella   52

soups: butternut squash soup   7

   ham, leek and potato soup   18

   zero point soup   6

Spanish cod   31

spicy pork casserole   28

spicy turkey marrow   22

steak fajita   43

stew, Moroccan vegetable   10

strawberry alaskas, baked   58

tagine, Moroccan chicken   53

toffee apple wedges   16

tomato and basil risotto   30

tomato tartlets, oven-roasted   9

tropical fruit crumble   59

tuna cakes with spring onion salsa   21

turkey: spicy turkey marrow   22

   turkey tomato pasta   44

vegetable lasagne   32

zero point soup   6